OUR AMAZING CONTINENTS

Continents are the largest pieces of land
on Earth. There are seven continents.
The largest is Asia. The other continents,
from largest to smallest, are Africa,
North America, South America, Antarctica,
Europe, and Australia. Each continent's
landscape has shaped the lives of its
animals, plants, and people.

Library of Congress Cataloging-in-Publication Data

Sayre, April Pulley.
Welcome to North America! / April Pulley Sayre.
    p. cm.—(Our amazing continents)
Summary: Introduces the continent of North America, looking at its
geography, plant and animal life, weather, and settlement by humans.
ISBN 0-7613-2150-0 (lib. bdg.)
1. North America—Juvenile literature. [1. North America.]   I. Title.

E38.5 .S395   2003
917—dc21   2002015419

Front cover photograph courtesy of Animals Animals/Earth Scenes
(© Erwin & Peggy Bauer); Back cover photograph courtesy of Photo
Researchers, Inc. (© Tom & Pat Leeson)

Map on p. 32 by Joe LeMonnier

Photographs courtesy of NASA: p. 1; Animals Animals/Earth Scenes: pp. 3
(© Gary Crabbe), 5 (right: © Richard Kolar), 13 (top: © Norbert Rosing),
19 (top right: © Stefano Nicolini; bottom right: © Michael Fogden), 20
(© John Lemker), 21 (right: © Tom Lazar), 25 (© Mickey Gibson), 27 (left:
© Allen Blake Sheldon; top right: © John Lemker); Photo Researchers,
Inc.: pp. 4 (© B. & C. Alexander), 5 (left: © Michael P. Gadomski), 13
(bottom: © Fletcher & Baylis), 18 (© Simon Fraser/SPL), 19 (left: © John
Eastcott & Yva Momatiuk), 22 (© John Eastcott & Yva Momatiuk), 23
(top: © Pat & Tom Leeson; bottom: © Paul J. Fusco), 26 (© Dan Suzio), 27
(bottom right: © Maslowski), 28 (© Lawrence Migdale); Photri, Inc.: p. 6;
Peter Arnold, Inc.: pp. 8 (© O. Langrand/ BIOS), 9 (© Secret Sea Visions),
12 (© Bruno J. Zehnder), 14 (top: © Vincent Keane); 15 (© S. J.
Krasemann); 24 (© Secret Sea Visions); Corbis: pp. 10 (© Bettmann), 11
(all: © Michael & Patricia Fogden), 14 (bottom: © Owen Franken), 17
(top right: © Dale C. Sparta; bottom right: © Raymond Gehman), 21
(left: © Nathan Benn), 29 (left: © Ariel Skelley; right: © Tom Stewart);
Woodfin Camp & Associates: pp. 16-17 (© John Eastcott & Yva
Momatiuk), 23 (middle: © Robert Frerck), 30-31 (© Robert Frerck).

Published by The Millbrook Press
2 Old New Milford Road
Brookfield, CT 06804
www.millbrookpress.com

**Fall colors at sunrise in the
mountains of New Hampshire**

WELCOME TO NORTH AMERICA!

APRIL PULLEY SAYRE

THE MILLBROOK PRESS, BROOKFIELD, CONNECTICUT

Greenland glacier

North America has lots of places to explore.

Coast of Maine

Powwow competition

In North America, you can kayak through the cold waters off of Maine's rocky coast. You can hike to a glacier in Greenland. You can enjoy a powwow in Alberta. Or you might see a show or go shopping in New York City, Mexico City, or Toronto.

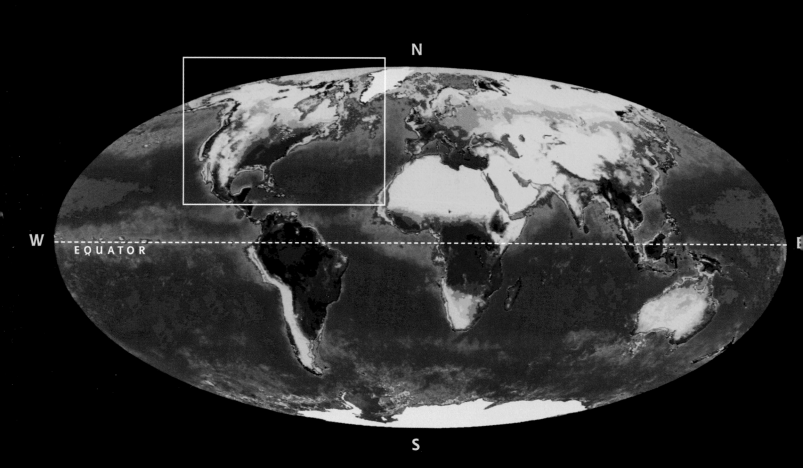

North America is the third-largest continent.

North America lies between the cold Arctic Ocean to the north, the warm Caribbean Sea to the south, the Pacific Ocean to the west, and the Atlantic Ocean to the east. An underwater rock shelf connects the continent to the island of Greenland, some Canadian islands, and the islands of the West Indies.

North America
is not a country.

Greenland is part of North America, but it i
controlled by Denmark, a country in Europe

A country is an area of land controlled by a government. North America has many countries, including Canada, Mexico, and the United States. Central America is a region that is part of the North American continent. Central America is a group of countries: Guatemala, Belize, Honduras, El Salvador, Nicaragua, Costa Rica, and Panama.

Exploring the coral reef off the shore of Mexico

Ships wait their turn to enter the locks on the canal

Panamanian golden frogs live in the tropical forests that line parts of the Panama Canal.

Red-eyed leaf frog

A three-toed sloth swimming to an island in the Panama Canal

The North American continent is just 31 miles (50 kilometers) wide in Panama.

People built the Panama Canal so that ships could travel between the Atlantic and Pacific oceans. Before the canal was built, ships had to sail all the way around the southern tip of South America to get from one ocean to another.

The northern part of North America is very wide.

It is about 4,000 miles (6,437 kilometers) from Alaska across Canada to Greenland. Greenland, the world's largest island, is mostly covered by glaciers. There are many glaciers in Canada and Alaska, too.

A glacier is a slow-moving river of ice

This far north the land is polar desert, arctic tundra, or taiga.

Polar bears

The weather is cold much of the year, but many animals and plants can still survive in the chilly conditions. Arctic foxes and polar bears hunt on the dry, icy polar desert. Musk oxen and caribou graze on the low-growing plants of the treeless tundra. Moose, bear, and wolverines live among the evergreen trees of the taiga.

Musk ox

Appalachian Mountains

Bear cubs learning to climb in the
Appalachian woods of North Carolina

North America
has mountains.

Some of the mountains in Central America and Mexico are active volcanoes.

North America has two large chains of mountains. One is in the East. One is in the West. The eastern mountains are the Appalachians. The western mountains, which stretch from Alaska to Panama, and then into South America, have no single name. The Mackenzie, Rocky, and Sierra Madres mountains are part of this mountain range—the longest and widest chain of mountains on Earth.

In between the two
groups of mountains are
North America's prairies.

Short-grass prairie, Canada

Geese take flight from a prairie pothole.

Prairie dogs

Prairies are grasslands. Tallgrass prairie has beautiful flowers and grass tall enough to hide a person! Short-grass prairies are home to prairie dogs, black-footed ferrets, and golden eagles. Some prairie land has small lakes, called potholes, which provide a place for ducks to raise their young. Much of the prairie has been turned into farms and ranch land.

North America has many kinds of forests.

Taiga is a type of forest that has many conifers such as spruce, fir, and pine. Conifers form their seeds inside cones. Taigas are found in Canada and Alaska. Farther south and east are temperate deciduous forests. Their trees have leaves that are broad and turn beautiful colors in the fall. Temperate rain forests grow in Oregon and British Columbia. Temperate rain forests have rainy, cool weather. In Mexico and Central America, tropical rain forests grow. Mexico and Central America are closer to the equator. This means it is warmer there than the rest of North America. The rain forests there have rainy, warm weather.

Temperate Rain Forest

In the fall, monarch butterflies migrate to another kind of forest, the fir forests, in the mountains of Mexico.

Monarch Butterflies

The fall colors of a deciduous forest

Double waterfall in a tropical rainforest in Costa Rica

North America has rivers, lakes, and streams.

Lake Huron

Mississippi River

The longest river in North America is the Mississippi. The winding Mississippi River forms the boundaries of many states.

The largest lake on Earth is Lake Superior, one of the five Great Lakes. The other Great Lakes are Michigan, Huron, Erie, and Ontario. These lakes are so large they have waves, beaches, and dunes, much like the ocean. But the water is freshwater—not salty, like ocean water.

Lake Michigan

Atchafalaya swamp, Louisiana

Shorebirds during spring migration

North America has wetlands, too.

Marshes, swamps, and bogs are wetlands. Frogs, fish, herons, and many other creatures feed in wetlands. Wetlands are natural sponges. They help hold water when it rains, preventing flooding in other places.

Cattle grazing in wetlands

Salt marsh

A diver swims past an Elephant Ear sponge in a coral reef.

North America also has islands and coral reefs.

The warm tropical islands of the West Indies are part of North America. There are over seven thousand of these islands, including the Bahamas, Cuba, Jamaica, and Puerto Rico. Some of the islands are the tops of mountains that have sunk into the sea.

Many islands have fringes of coral called reefs. Coral reefs are limestone made by coral animals. Schools of colorful fish swim around the corals.

A mangrove swamp on the island of Belize

Parts of North America are covered by desert.

Sand dunes in the Mojave desert, in California

Desert is dry land. But most North American deserts are not as dry and bare as the Sahara in Africa. Cacti, ocotillo plants, and wildflowers grow in the Sonoran Desert. During the rainy season the prickly cacti store water in their stems. Then in the dry season, they can use it to survive. To stay cool, desert animals such as snakes and roadrunners do their hunting at night, out of the hot sun.

Saguaro cactus forest

Diamondback rattlesnake

Cactus wren

Apache family

North America is home to many people.

The descendants of the first people to live in North America are called Native Americans. In Canada, they are called First Nations. They belong to many different tribes, each with its own culture and customs. Many other people, from all over the world, have also settled in North America. North Americans speak English, Spanish, French, German, Tagalog, and many other languages.

Chicago

North America has big cities, small towns, and lots of highways.

It has malls, main streets, machinery, and millions of people. But underneath all this is the North American continent. And the continent's natural landscapes affect the lives of North Americans every day.

NORTH AMERICA

ASIA

ARCTIC OCEAN

Greenland

Arctic Circle

WESTERN MOUNTAIN RANGE

GULF OF ALASKA

Great Lakes
1 Lake Superior
2 Lake Michigan
3 Lake Huron
4 Lake Erie
5 Lake Ontario

KEY
- Tundra
- Taiga
- Prairie
- Humid
- Desert
- Mountain
- Cool Rain Forest
- Tropical Rain Forest

Mississippi River

APPALACHIANS

ATLANTIC OCEAN

Sonoran Desert

West Indies

Central America

CARIBBEAN SEA

0   400 miles
0   600 kilometers

PACIFIC OCEAN

Panama Canal

SOUTH AMERICA

How do you get to know the face of a continent?

Books are one way. This book is about the natural features of a continent. Maps are another way. You can discover the heights of mountains and the depths of valleys by looking at a topographical map. A political map will show you the outlines of countries and locations of cities and towns.

Globes are a third way to learn about the land you live on. Because globes are Earth-shaped, they show more accurately how big the continents are, and where they are. Maps show an Earth that is squashed flat, so the positions and sizes of continents are slightly distorted. A globe can help you imagine what an astronaut sees when looking at our planet from space. Perhaps one day you'll fly into space and see it for yourself! Then you can gaze down at the brown faces of continents, and the blue of the oceans, and the white clouds floating around Earth.